Breathe & Bloom 3

Flower Patterns

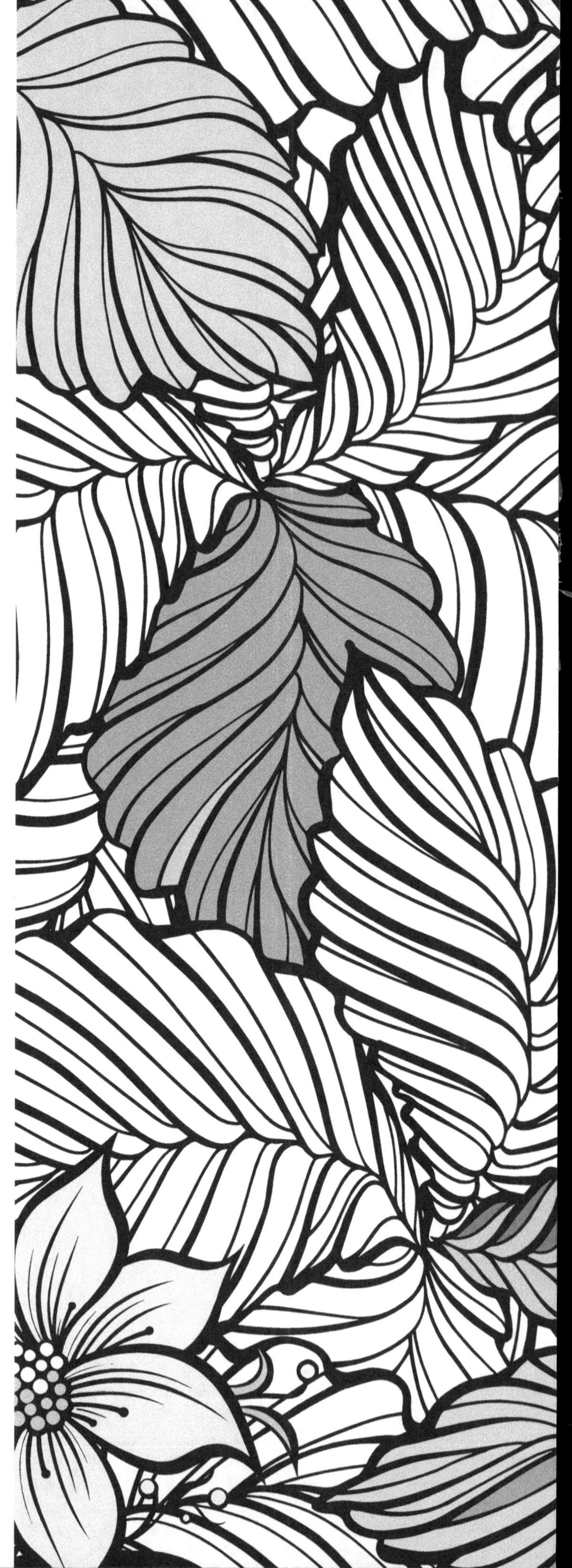

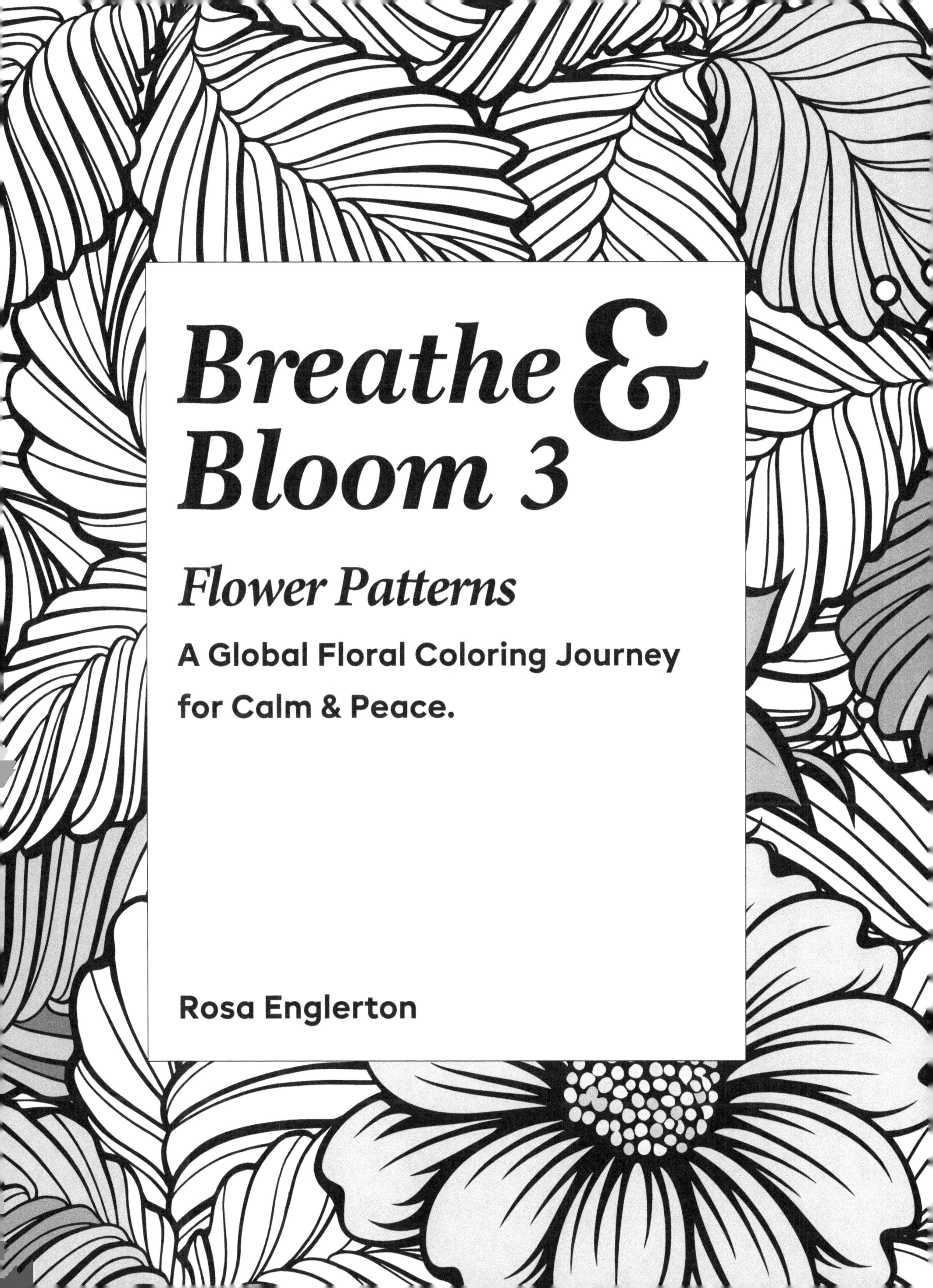

Breathe & Bloom 3

Flower Patterns

A Global Floral Coloring Journey for Calm & Peace.

Rosa Englerton

How to Use this Book

Hi and thank you for joining us in this journey of peace and relaxation.

This coloring book combines natural imagery with breathing exercises that help you return to return to ease and relaxation.

Help yourself affirms the right to rest and reset. Shifts your focus from being fixed to feeling free and elevated. Support yourself with mental clarity during chaotic moments. Reaffirm your will with agency during stress. Take a safe internal refuge. Restore your inner strength and balance.

The book has ten sections followed by ten-large size paintable flowers.

Start by reading the breathing exercise. Meditate on it for a few minutes, and start your breathing. Close your eyes. Look for the light of the Creator. Relax and put yourself in His hands.

Now you are ready to take your favourite coloring pencils, crayons, or markers, and let yourself flow into the flower and the colors. Be free. Imagine you are in the garden of Paradise. You are in control. The flower is your friend and is allowing you to give it the colors you want. Paint the background with patterns, or draw your own flowers.

When you are done painting, look at the flower, and do the breathing exercise again. If you have time, take a walk in the park. Look at the greenery, look at the flowers, see the colors in the world that surround you.

Breathe.

Everything is ok.
You are stronger now.

God Bless you!

Scent Imagination

Look at the flower on the opposite page.

- Close your eyes
- Imagine the scent of this flower
- Imagine its color

Cloud Thoughts

Sit quietly and imagine your thoughts as clouds drifting across the sky. Watch them come and go without clinging or pushing them away. Hang one of your worries to a cloud and blow them away.

Affirmation
Quote

Calm is not a destination. It's a breath I return to.

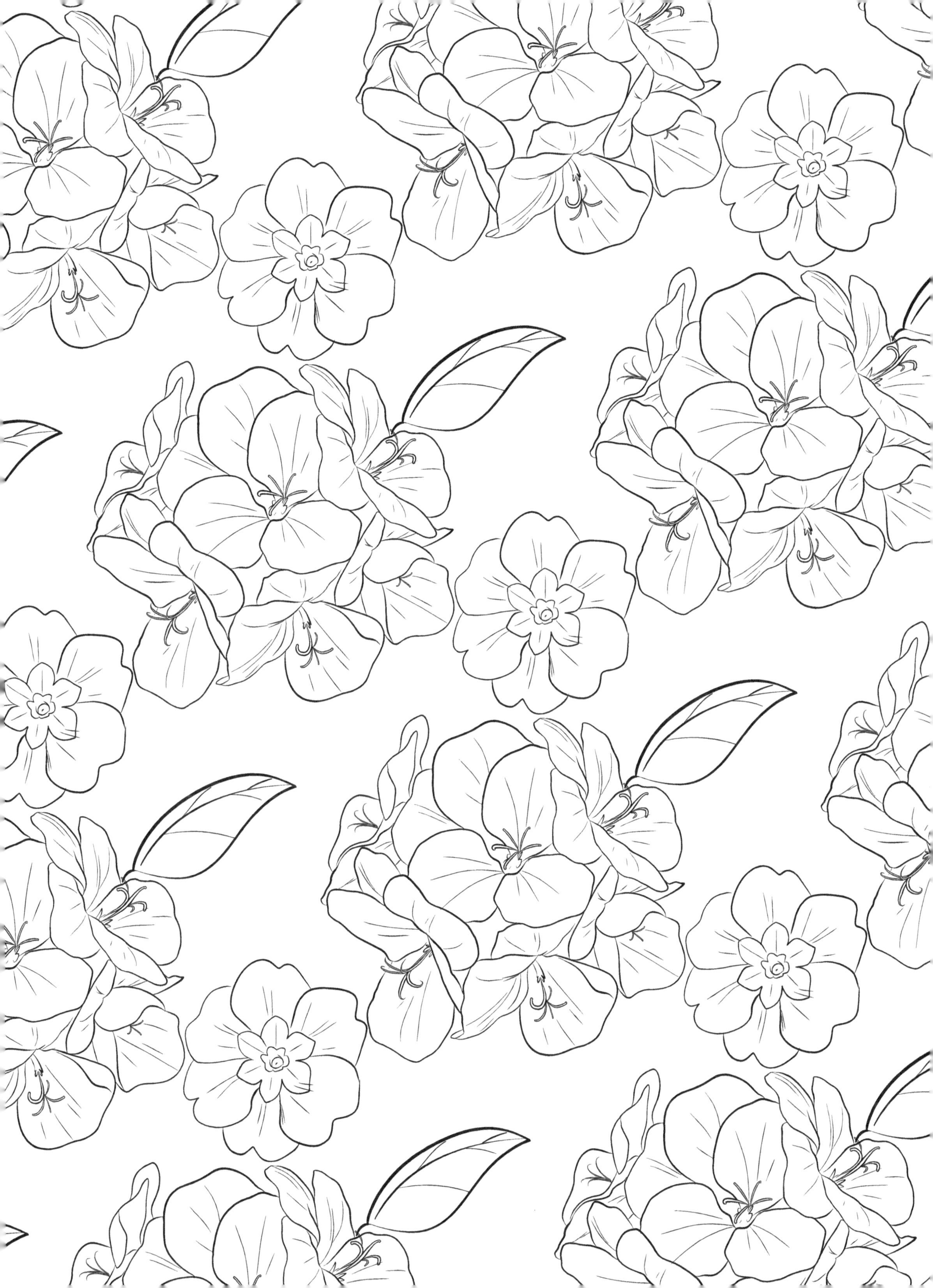

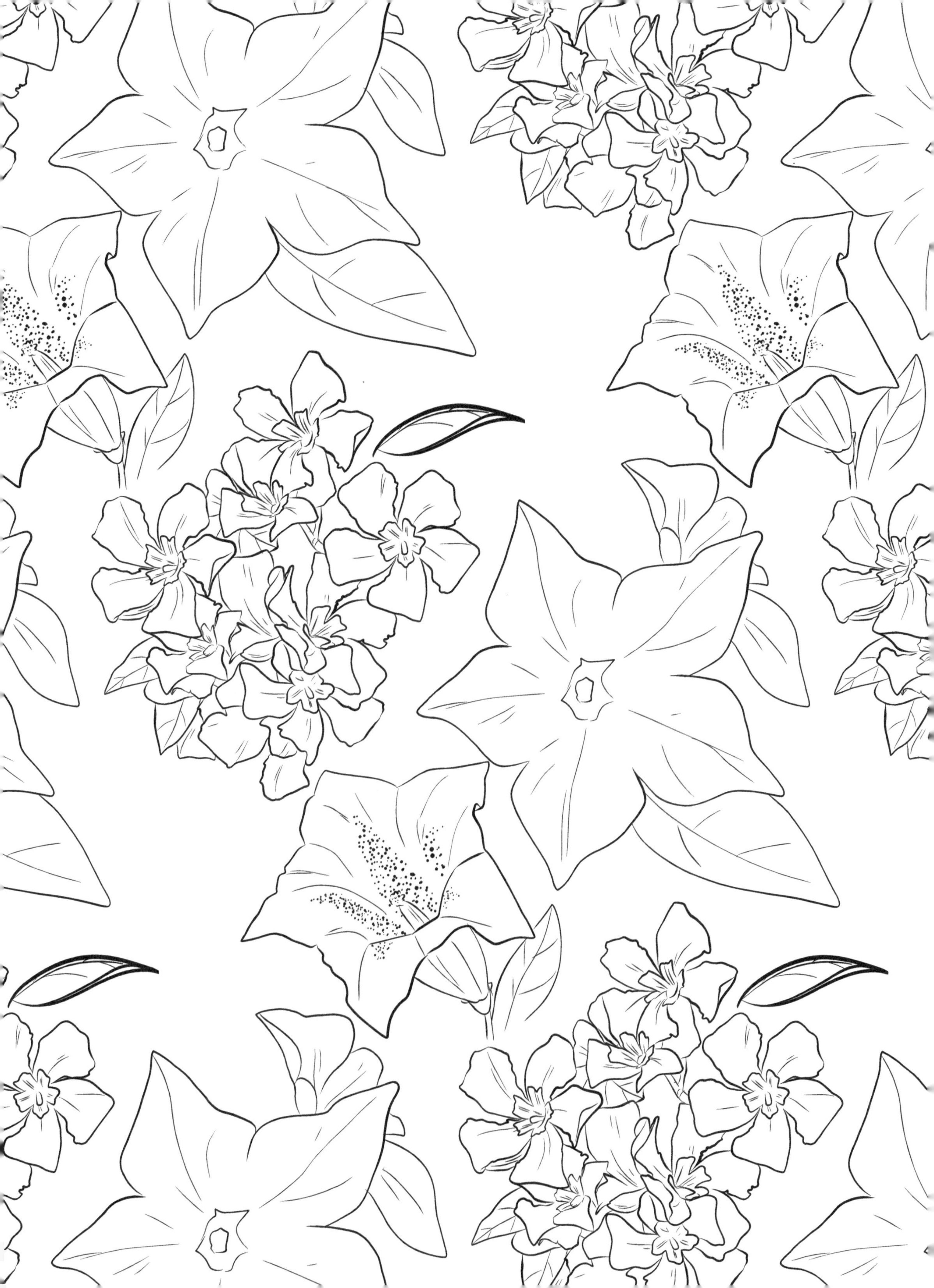

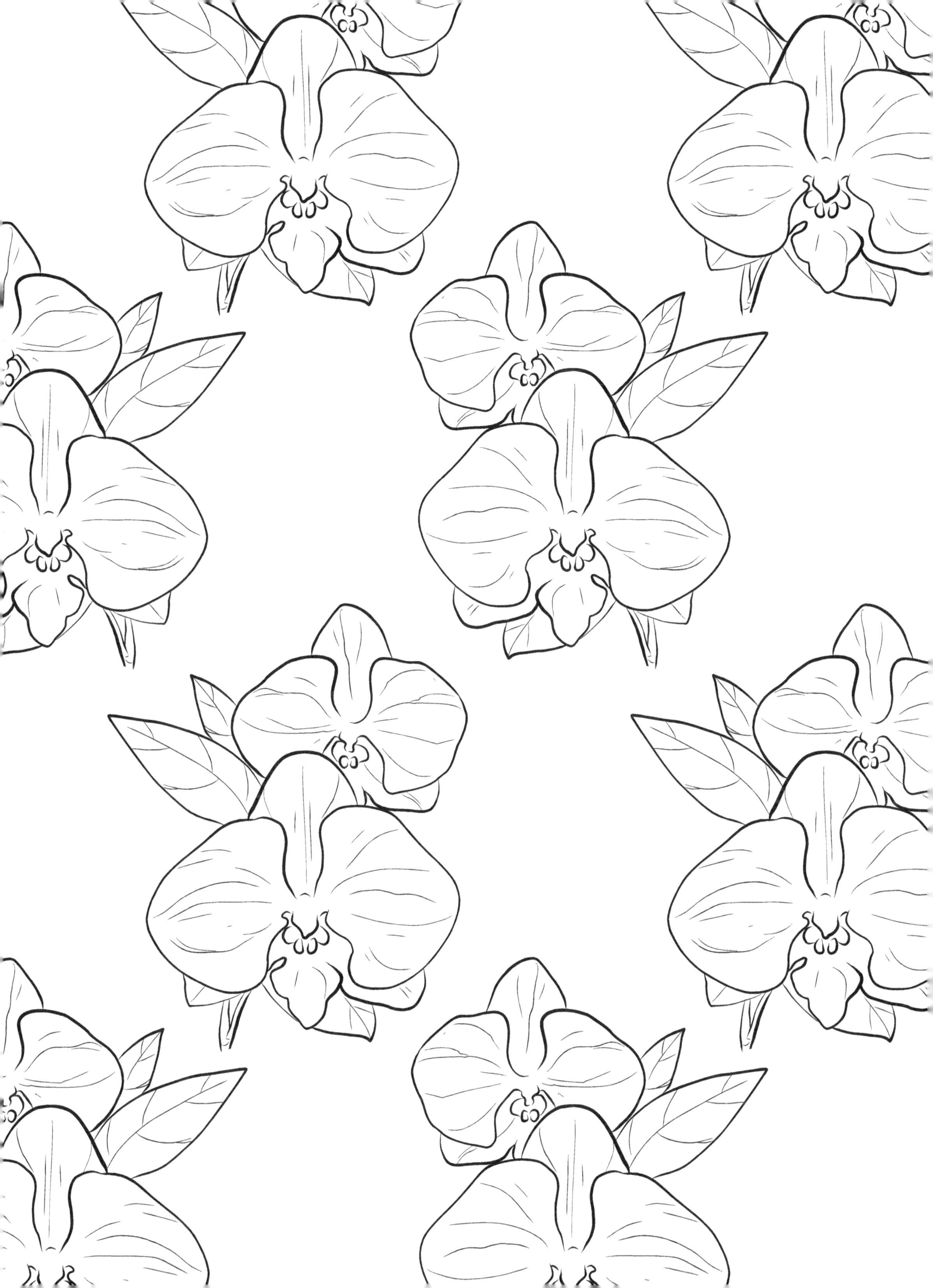

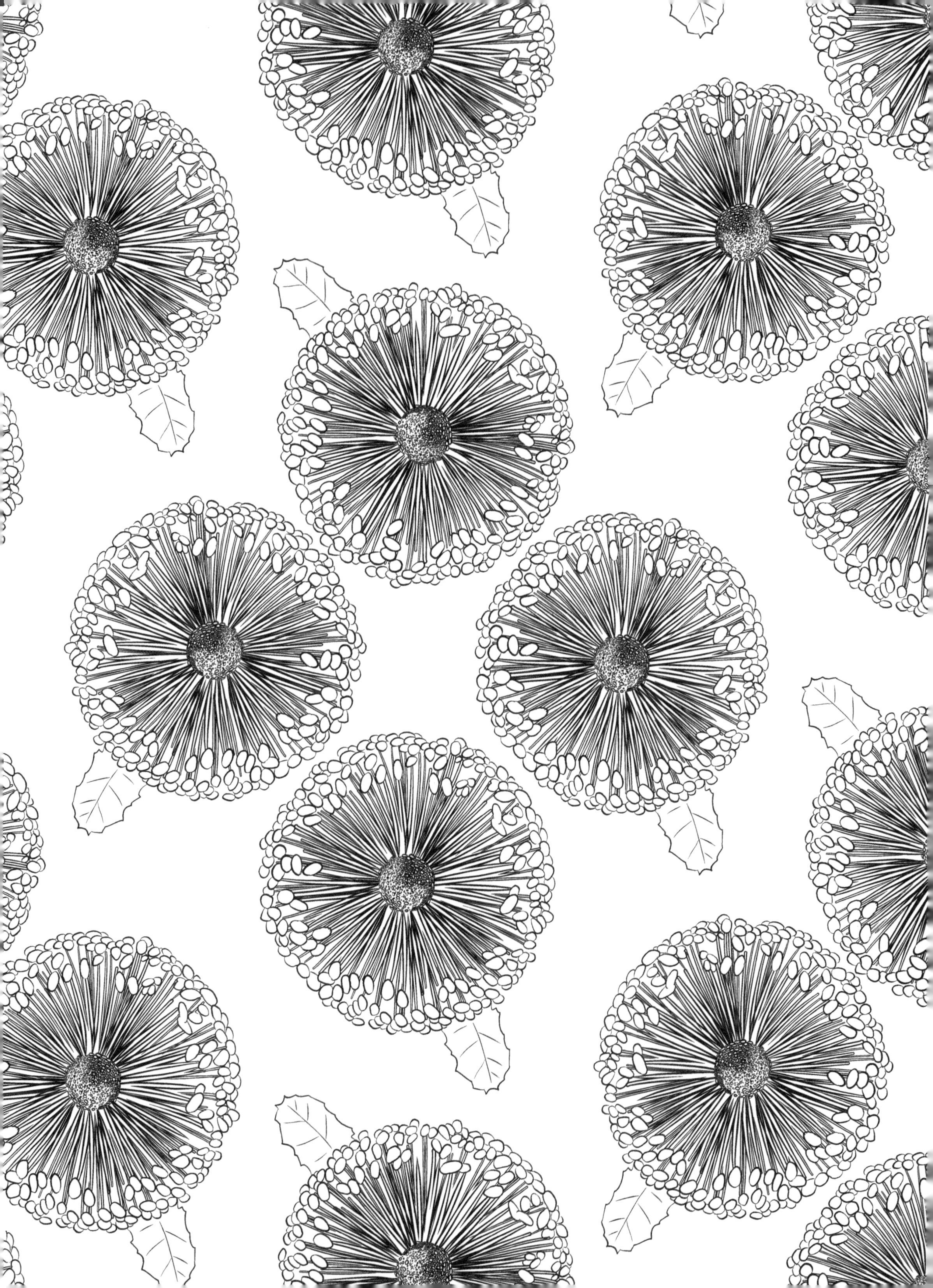

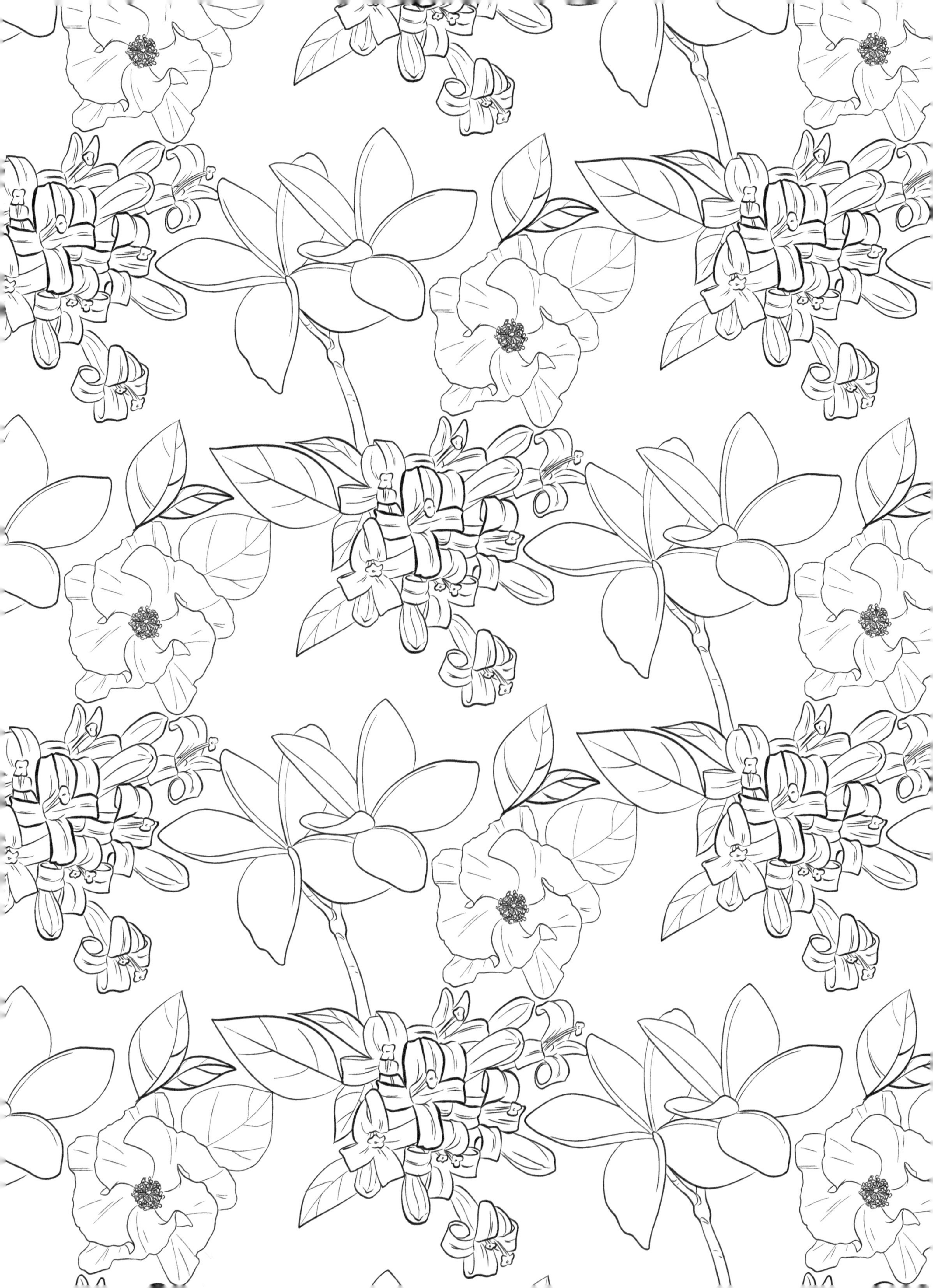

Scent Imagination

Look at the flower on the opposite page.

- Close your eyes
- Imagine the scent of this flower
- Imagine its color

Flower in Your Palm

Imagine holding a flower in your palm. Feel its weight, texture, and softness. It silky like your skin. Inhale slowly. Smelling its scent, and exhale gently.

Affirmation
Quote

I breathe in clarity.
I breathe out the noise.

I breath in freedom,
I breath out pain.

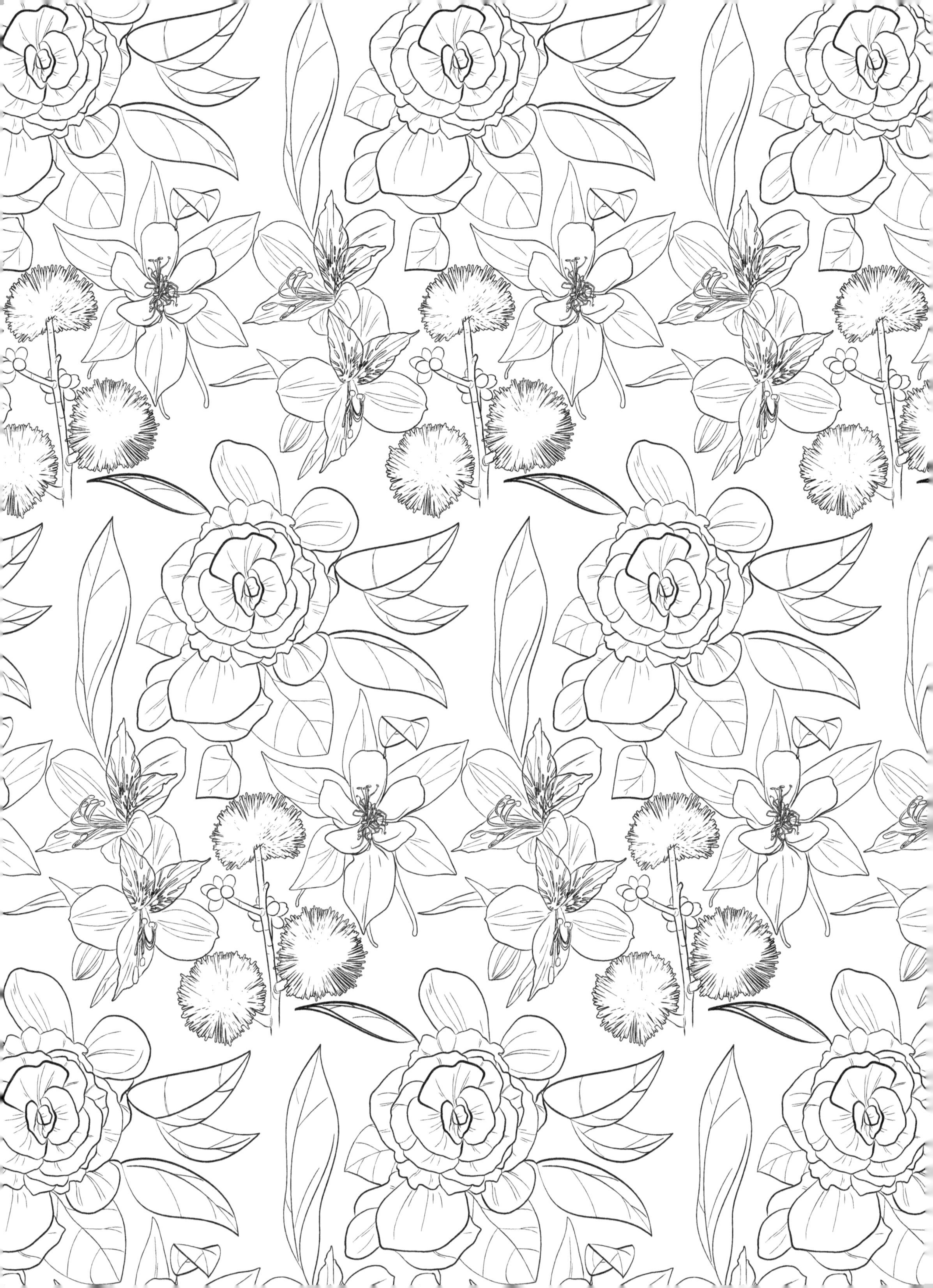

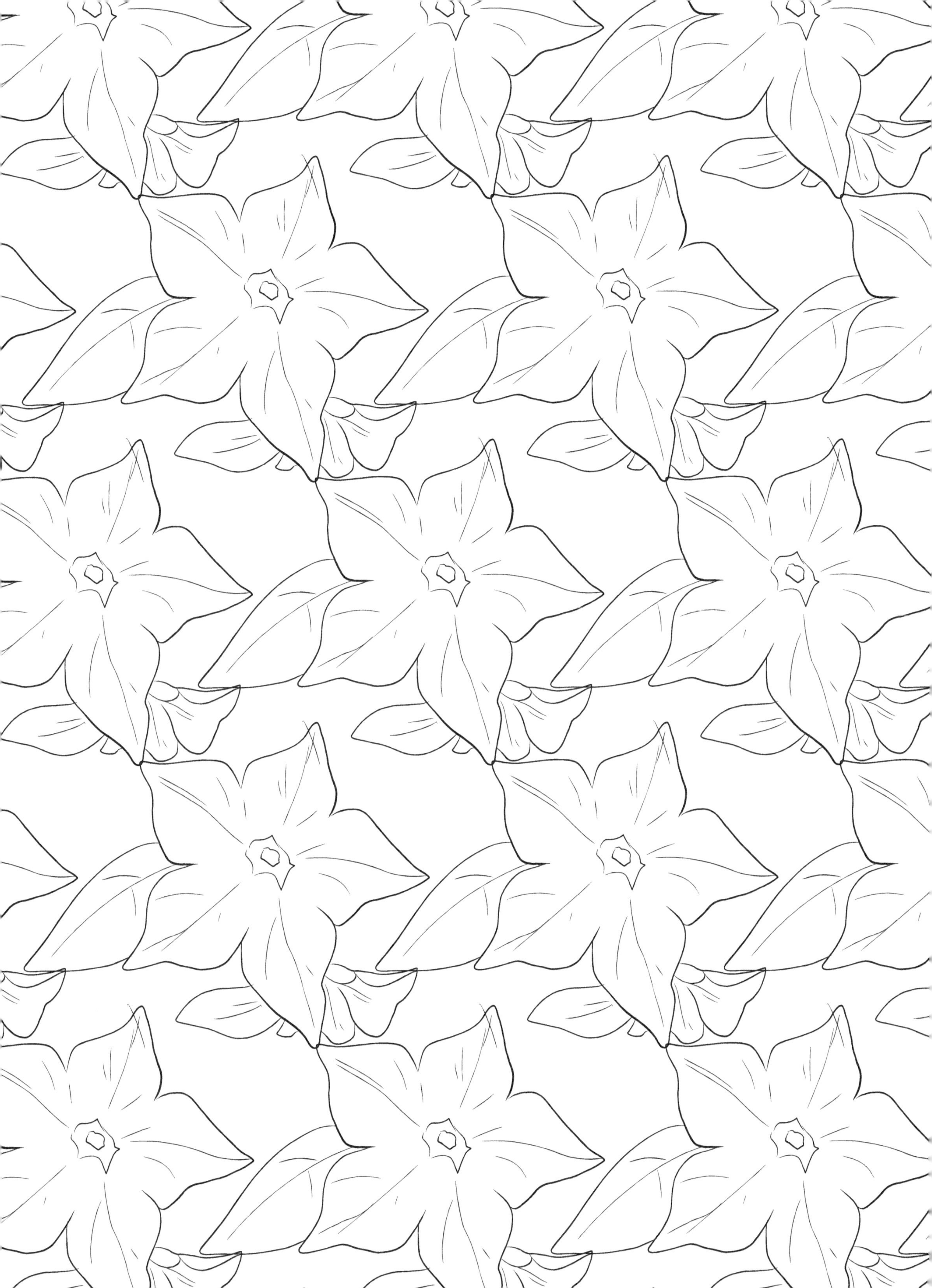

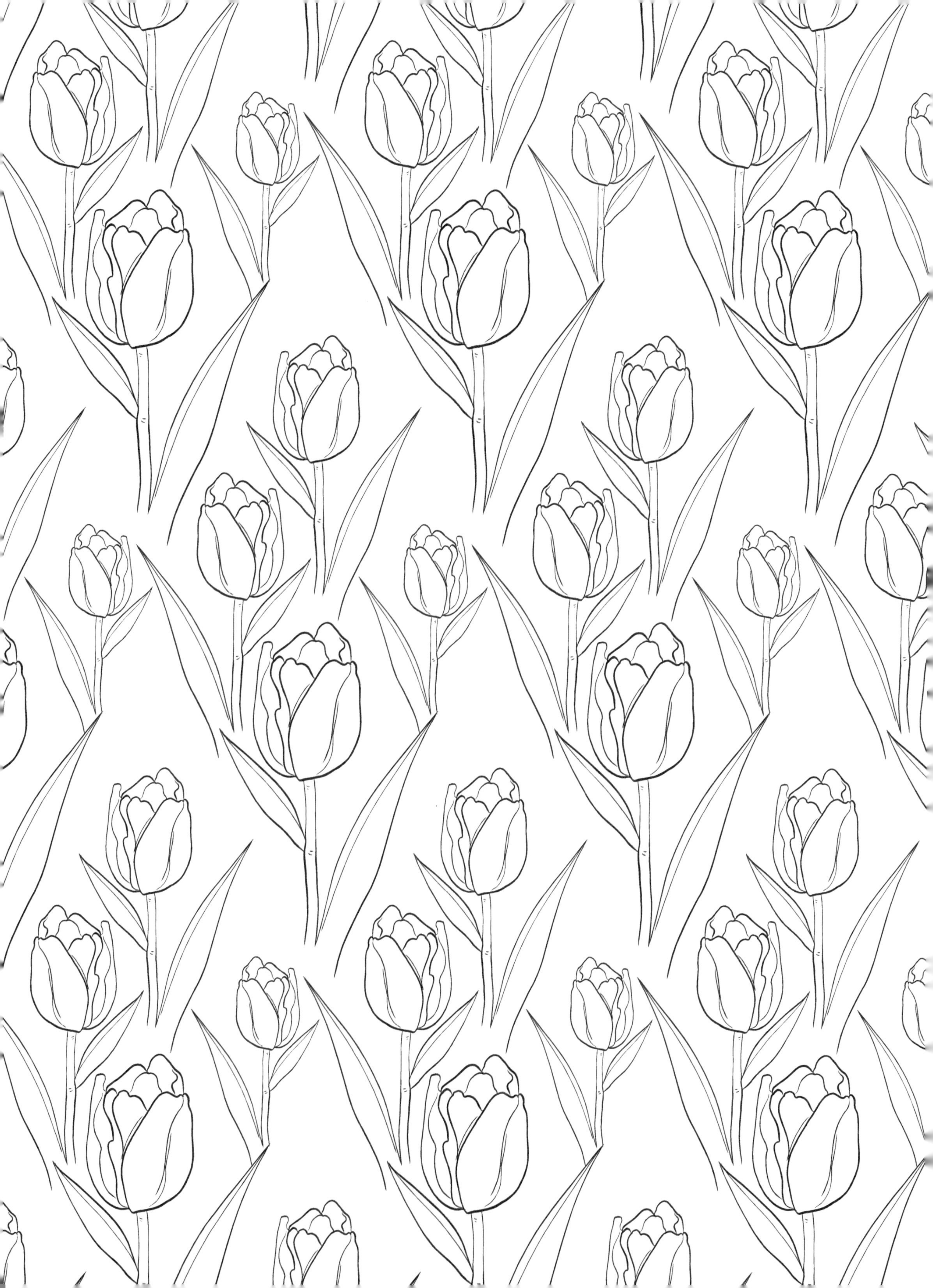

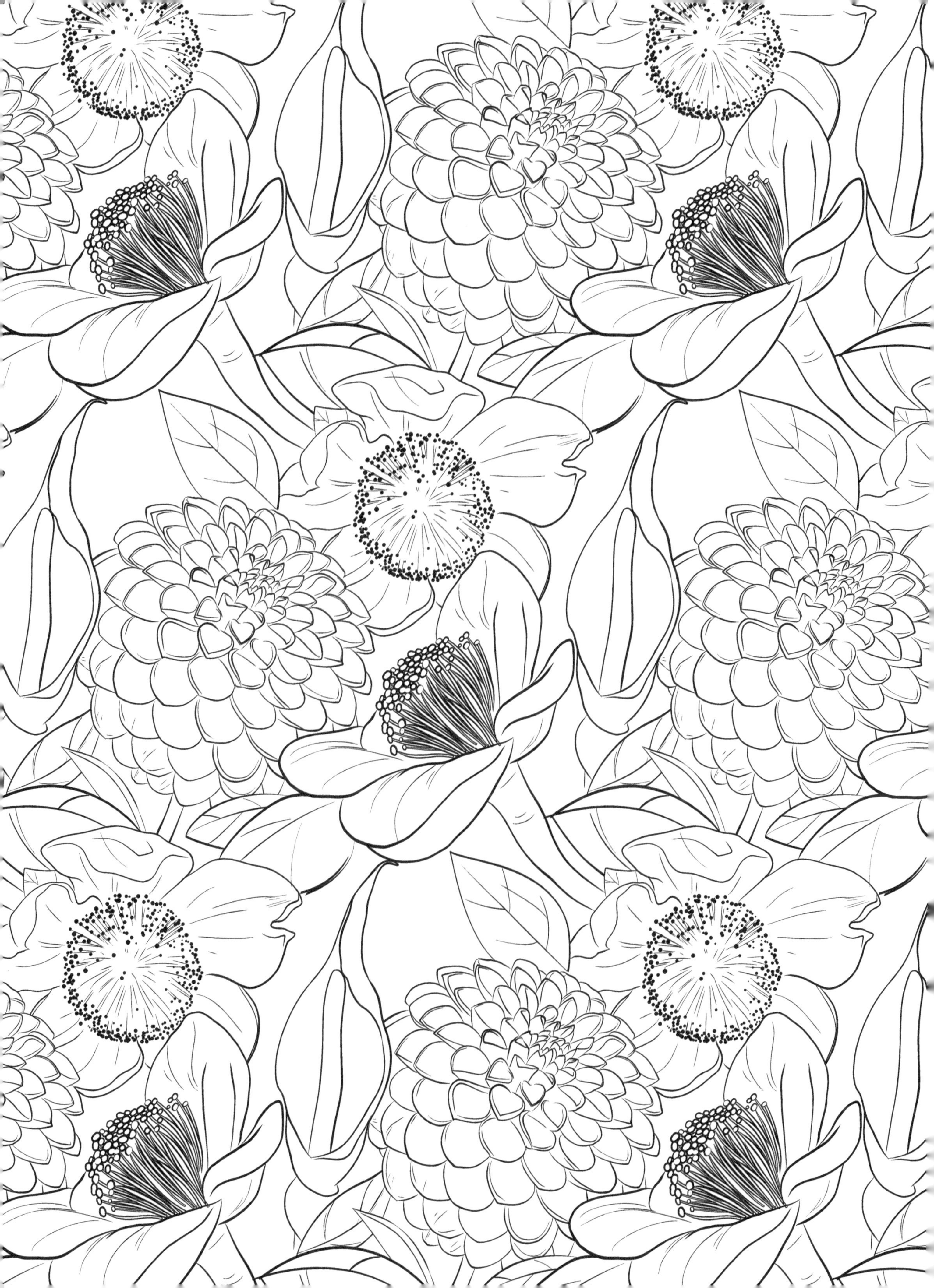

Scent Imagination

Look at the flower on the opposite page.

- Close your eyes
- Imagine the scent of this flower
- Imagine its color

The Reset Breath

Take one deep inhale (through the nose), hold for 2 seconds, and exhale with a long sigh. Do this just, intentionally. When you exhale, push out that worry. Push out that pain. Inhale the pure scent of Paradise.

Affirmation
Quote

Even now, I can choose stillness.

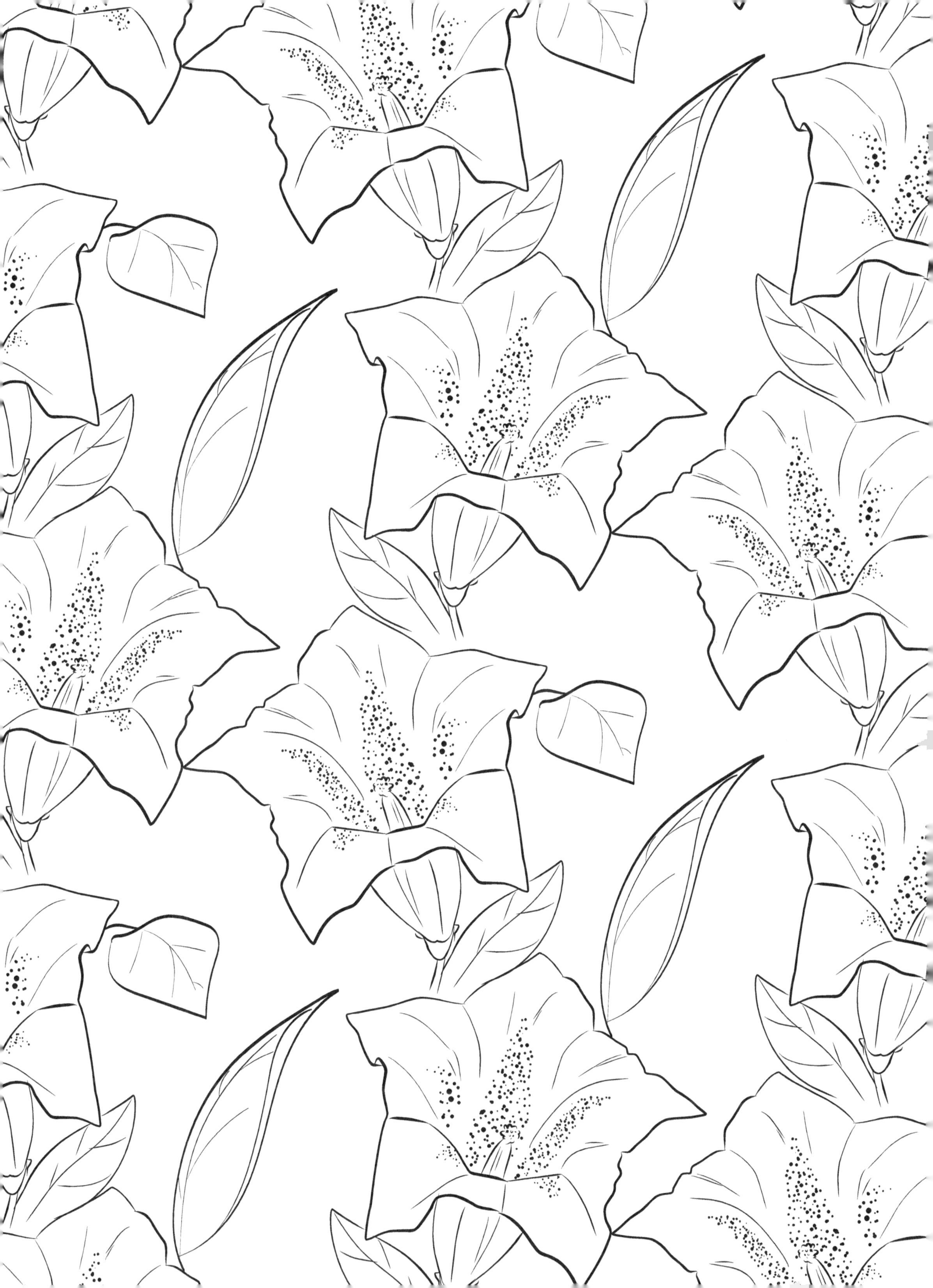

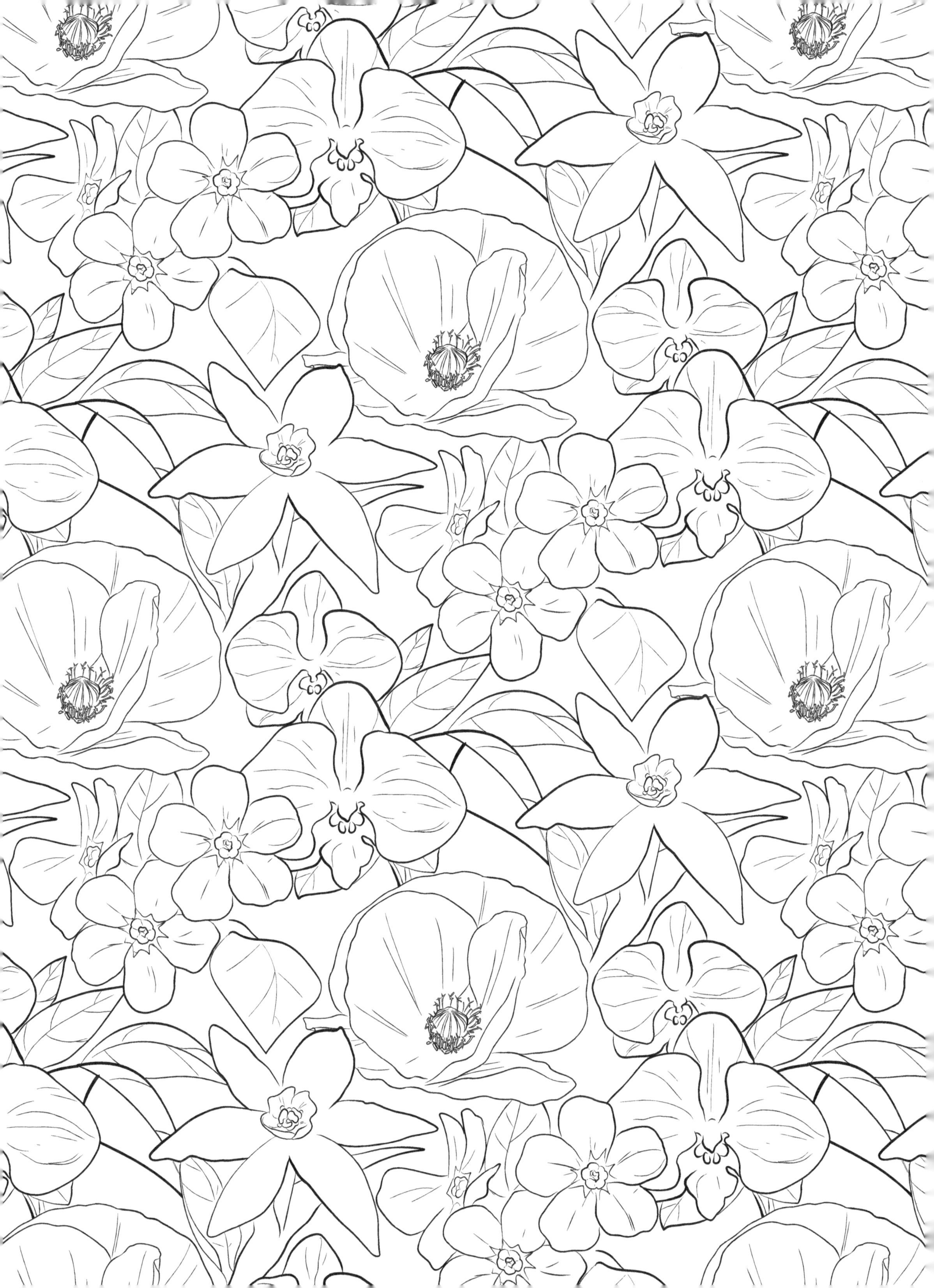

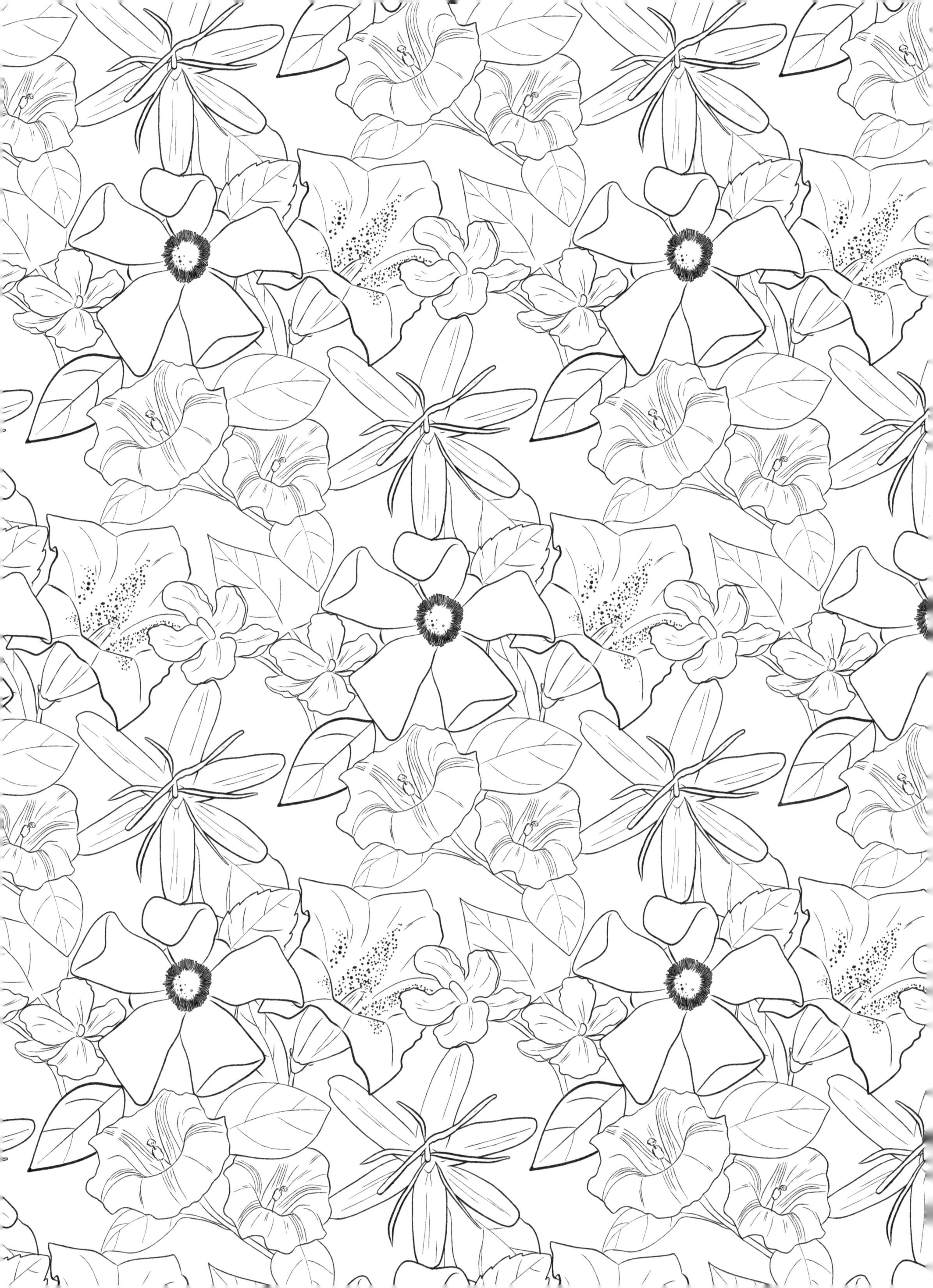

Scent Imagination

Look at the flower on the opposite page.

- Close your eyes
- Imagine the scent of this flower
- Imagine its color

Three Gratitude Breaths

With each of three deep breaths, silently name one thing you're grateful for. Big or small.

Affirmation
Quote

My breath is my shelter. I return to it when the world feels too loud, its soothing and peaceful.

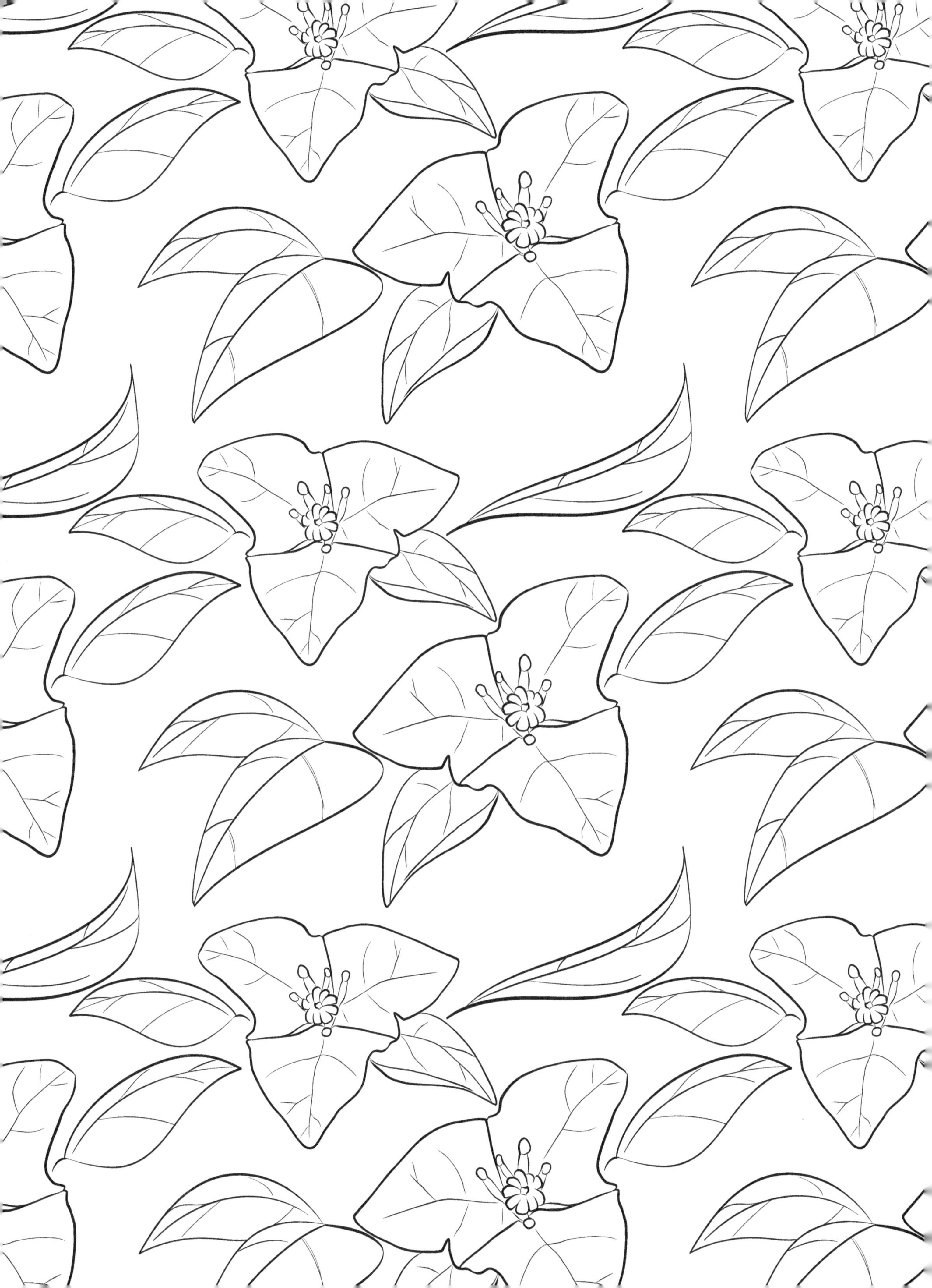

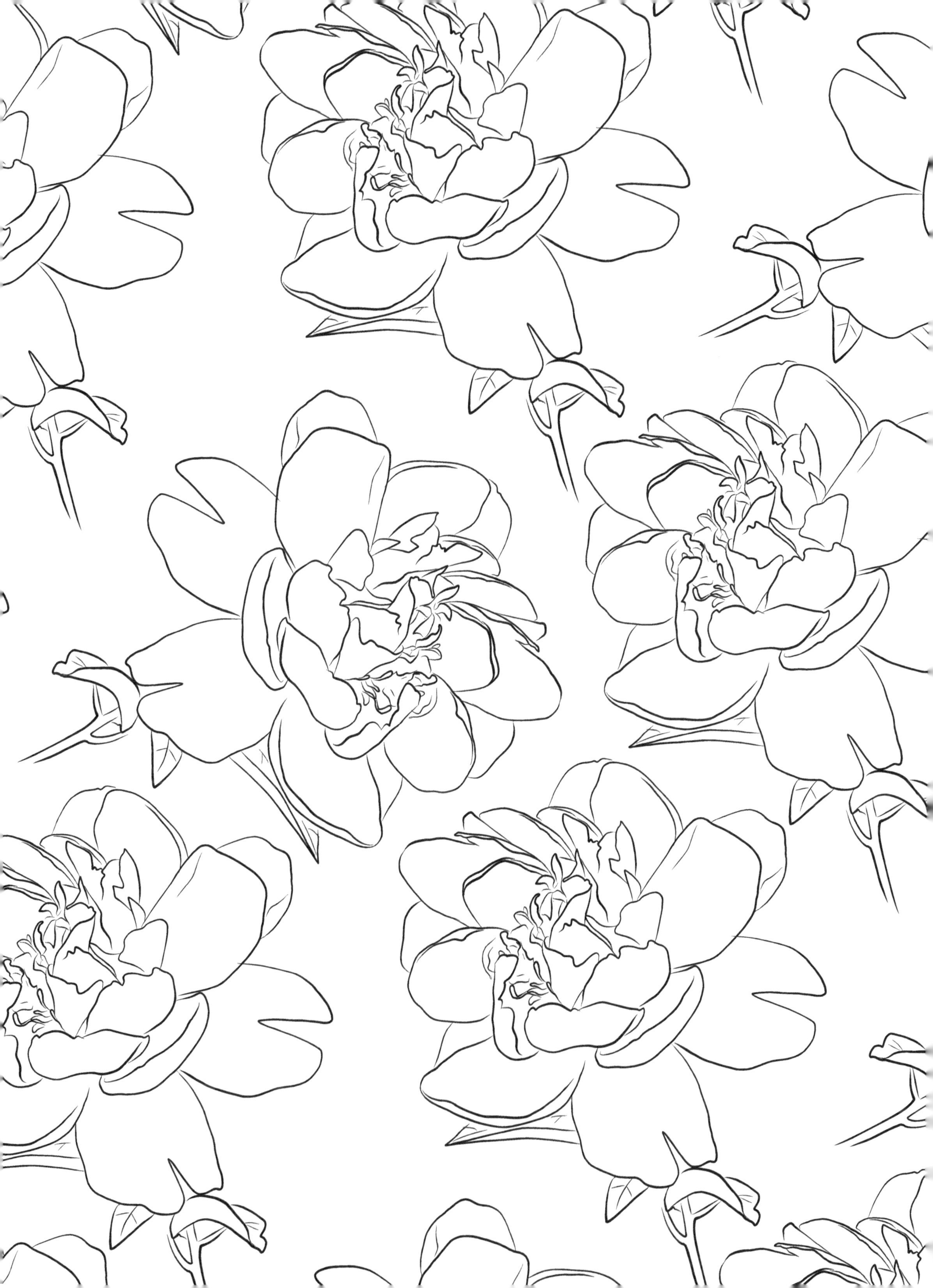

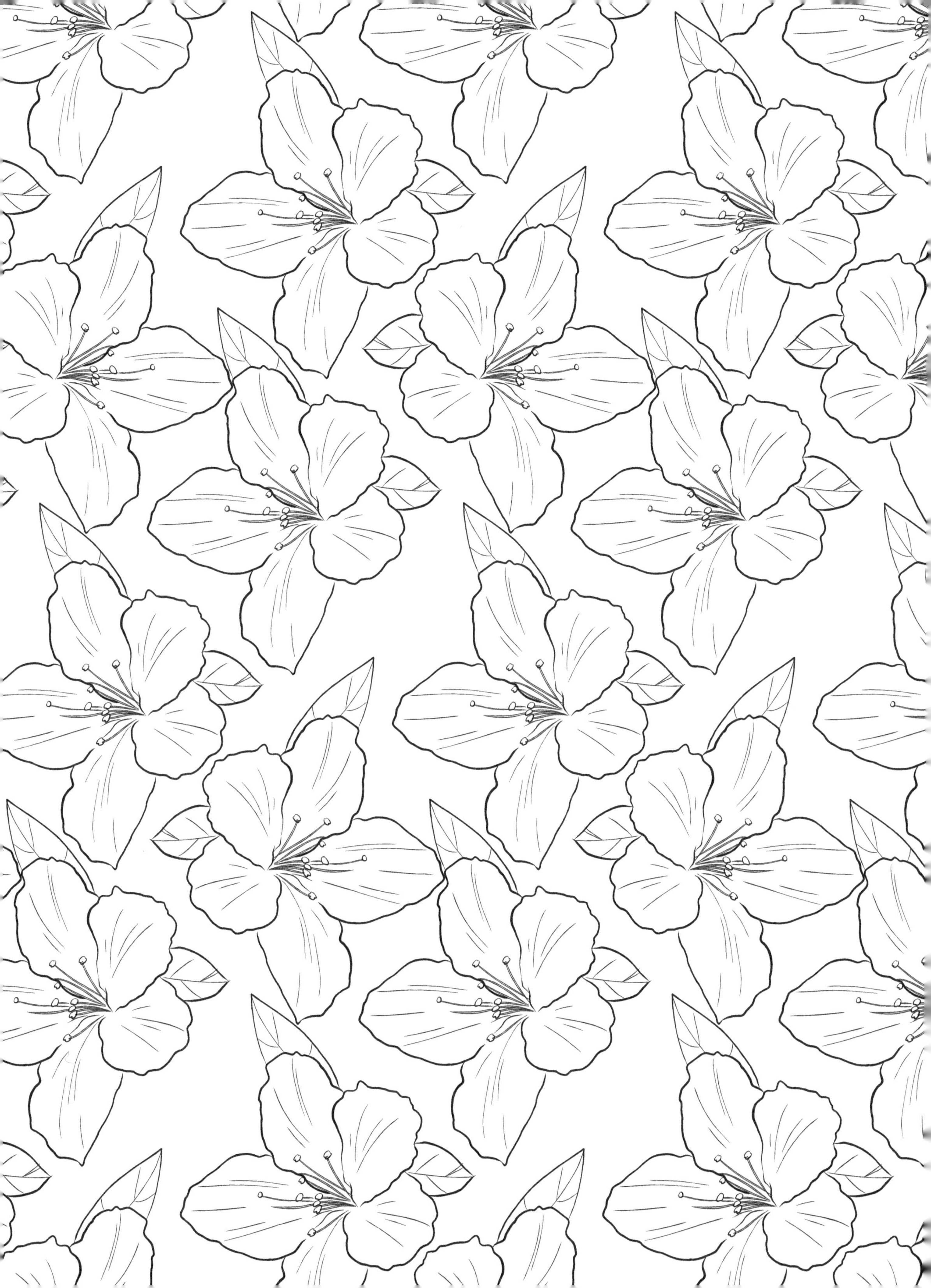

Scent Imagination

Look at the flower on the opposite page.

- Close your eyes
- Imagine the scent of this flower
- Imagine its color

Color Your Calm

Close your eyes, and as you visualize coloring, mentally say:

- *"I am here."*
- *"I am okay."*
- *"I am letting go."*

Affirmation
Quote

I am safe. I am steady. I am enough, I can go on with my life to new beautiful horizons.

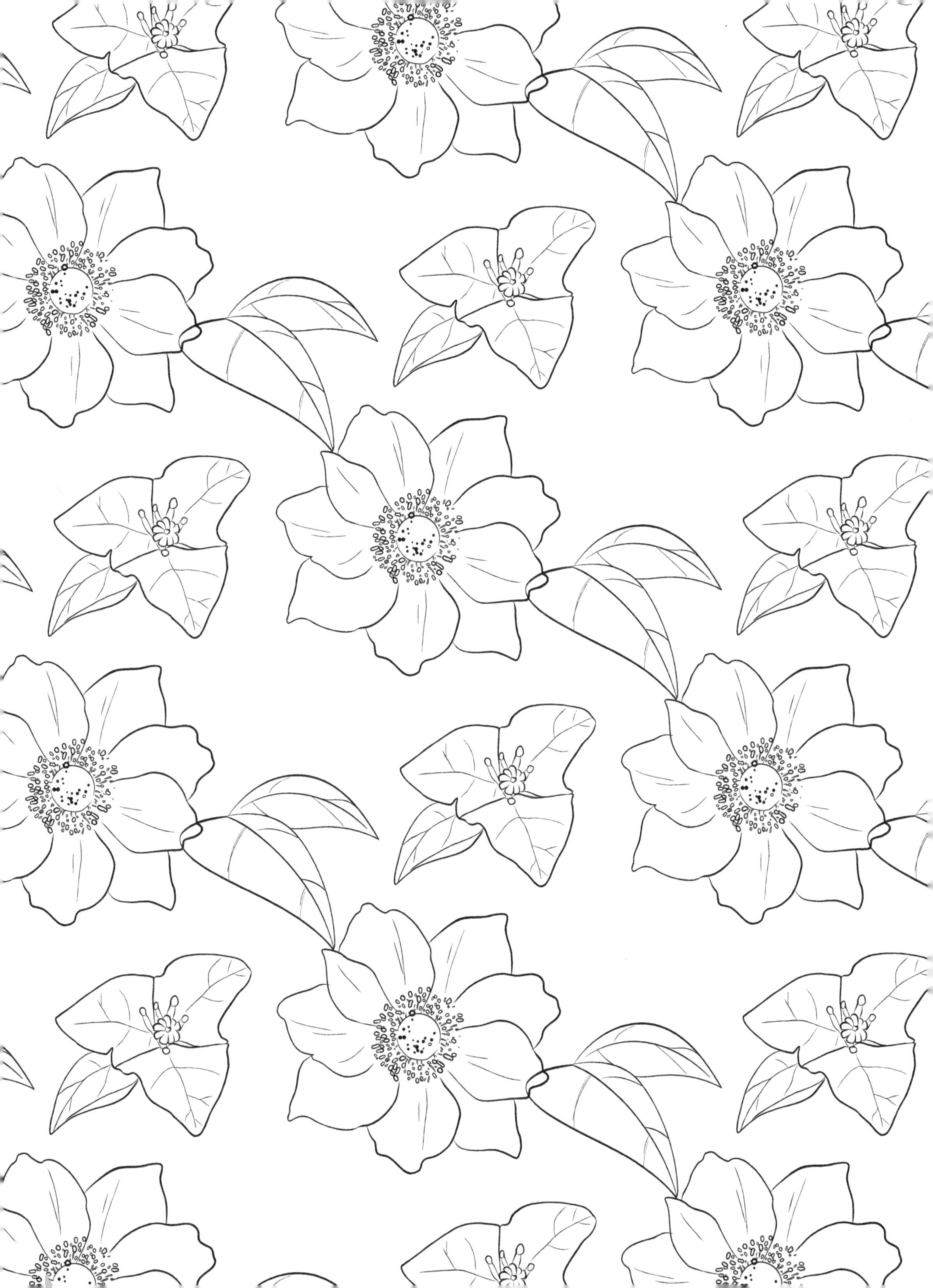

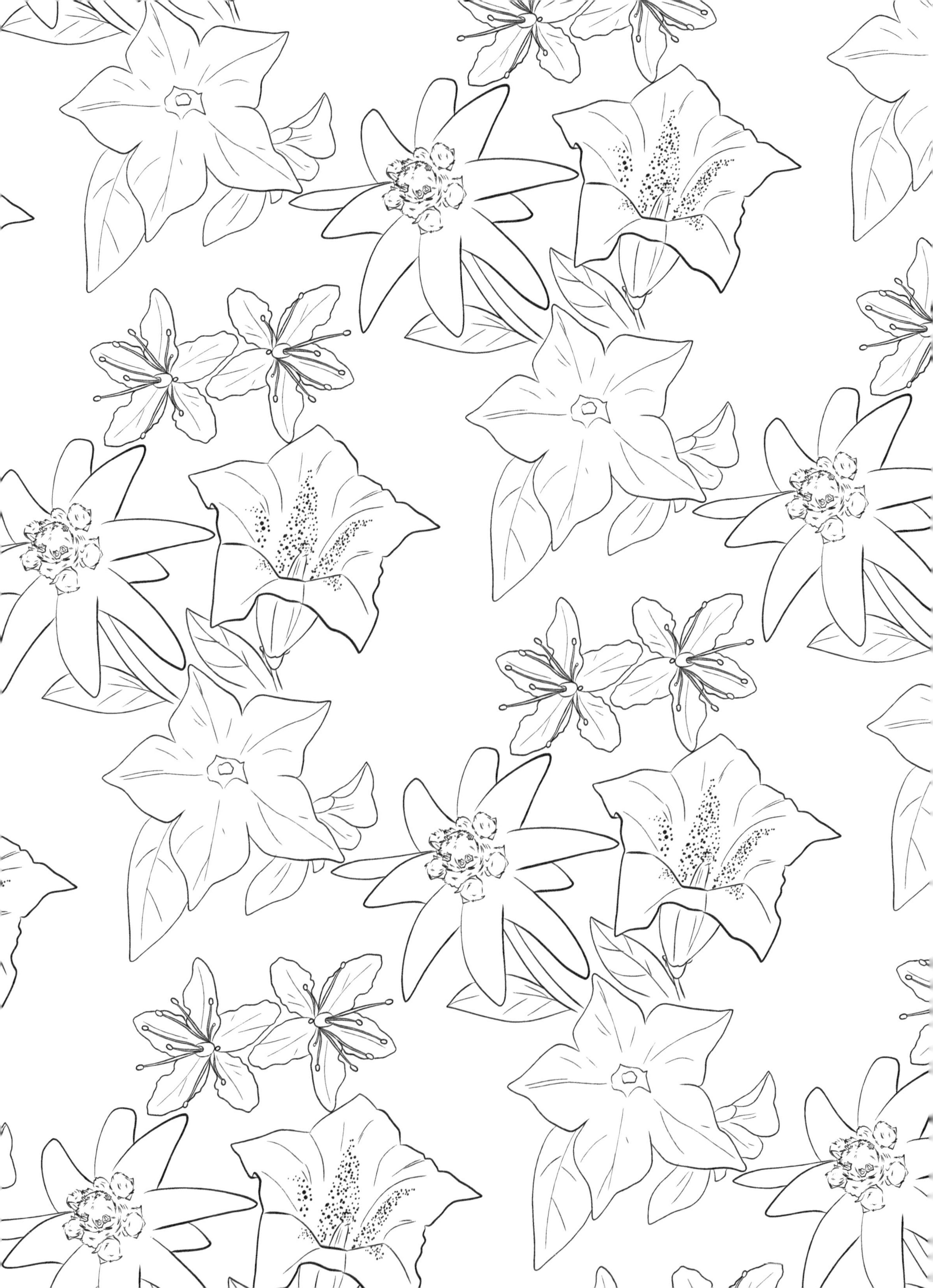

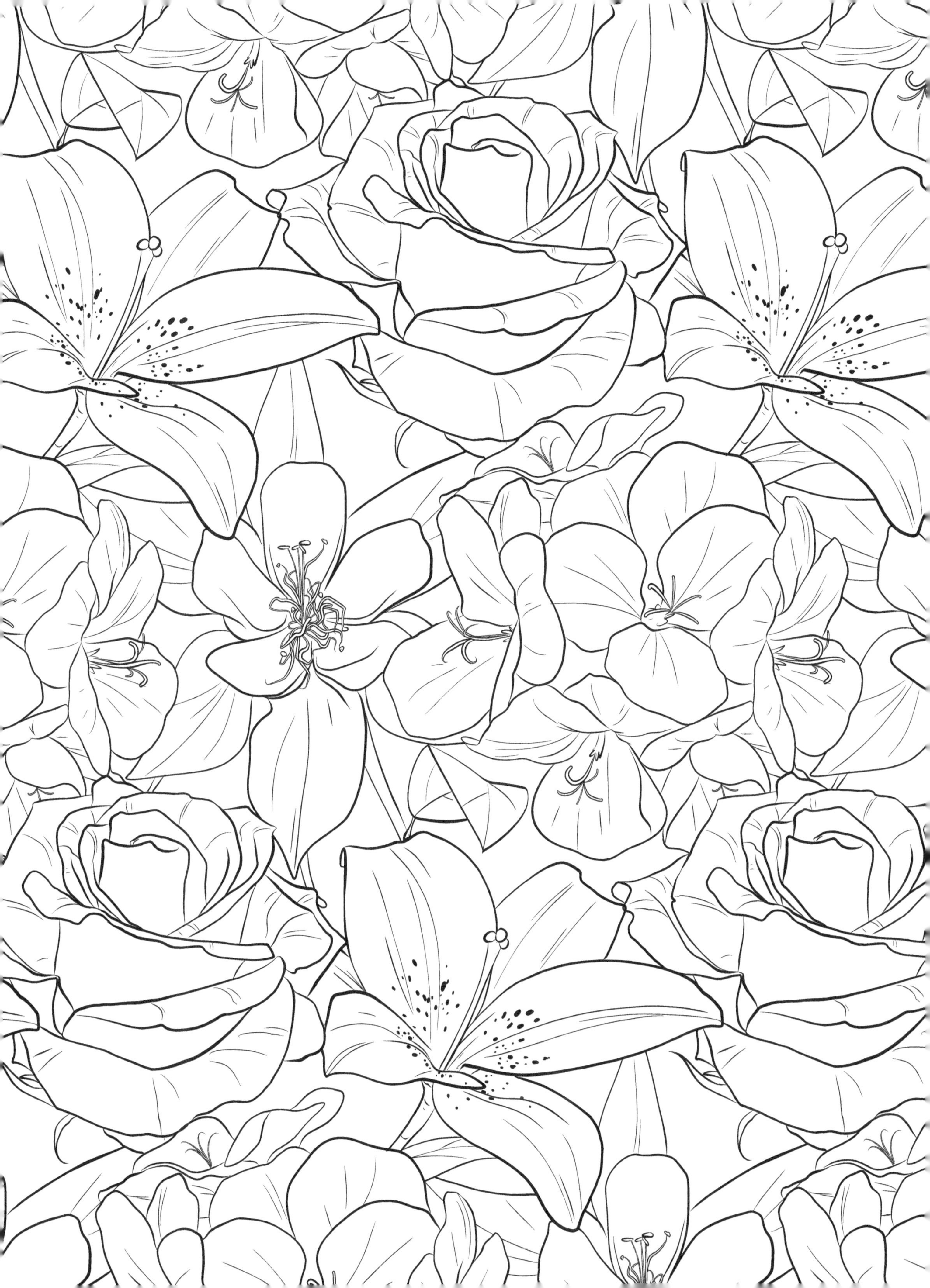

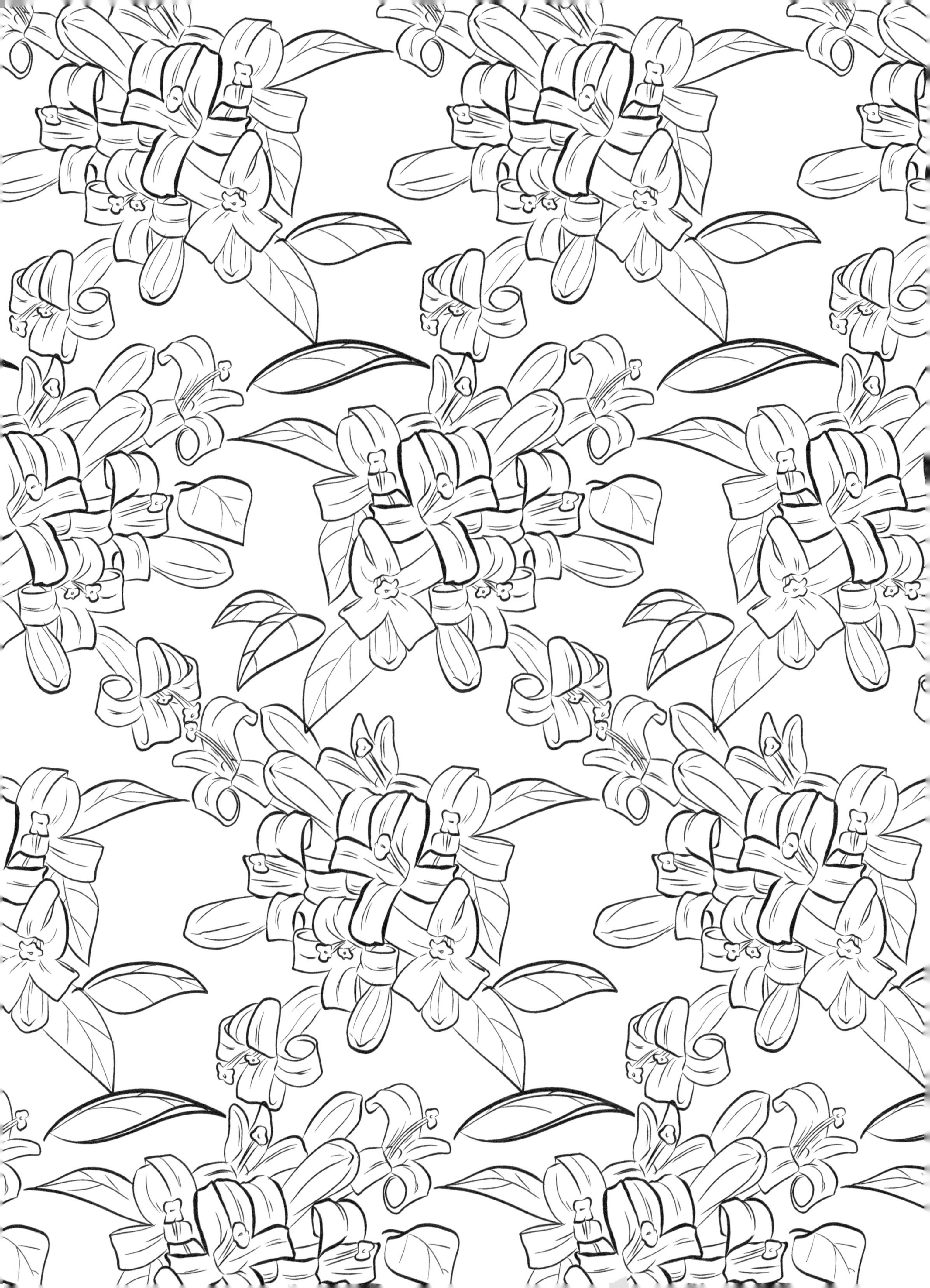

Peace